T0357907

What is Treasure?
What Do You Value?

Series Consultant: Linda Hoyt

Flying Start
to Literacy®

Contents

Introduction

What is treasure?   A chest full of coins? Rare and expensive jewels?

Coins, jewels and golden statues are certainly worth a lot of money, but sometimes the most treasured things have a different kind of value.

A treasure might be something that is valuable and important just to you, and something that might have no value to anyone else.

So, what is precious to you? What do you value? What do you think treasure is?

Treasure from the past

Have you ever visited a museum? Here are some of the things you might see.

Do you think these are treasure? Why?

Speak out!

Read what these students think of as treasure.

Treasure doesn't have to be gold or diamonds, like pirates' treasure. I have a little glass box that my grandma gave me when I was little. It's precious to me because it reminds me of her.

I think treasure is something you value and that you want to keep for your whole life.

My family is precious to me because my family loves and cares about me. They feed me and buy me stuff. They give me company and happiness. My family teaches me from their own experience.

It would be good to find lots of treasure and be really rich because you could help lots of people.

When I think of treasure, I think of gold and precious gems. But I don't think that many people do find that kind of treasure – it's just in books and in movies.

King Midas and the golden touch

Retold by Isabella Jose

In this story, King Midas changed his mind about what he thought of as treasure.   What made him change his mind?

King Midas loved gold. In his palace, he had rooms and rooms filled with gold. The only thing that he loved more than gold was his daughter.

One day, while the king was walking in his garden, he met an old man who was lost. The king recognised the old man as his teacher from long ago. He took the old man into the palace and gave him a huge feast.

"You have been so kind to me," said the old man. "To reward you, I will grant you a wish."

The king thought for a minute. "I wish that everything I touch would turn into gold," said King Midas.

"Are you sure this is what you want?" asked the old man.

"Of course!" said King Midas. "I will have more treasure than any other king."

And so the old man granted the wish!

King Midas touched his chair and it turned to gold. He touched his table and it turned to gold. As he walked through his palace, he touched the statues and they all turned to gold.

"This is wonderful," said King Midas. "Now I will have more gold than I ever dreamed of having."

But when he was hungry, King Midas made a terrible discovery. As soon as he touched his food, it turned to gold. And when he tried to drink some water, it, too, turned to gold.

"Don't worry, Father," said his daughter, and she threw her arms around him. Immediately, she turned into a golden statue.

"Oh no! What have I done?" cried King Midas.

The old man heard the king weeping for his beloved daughter.

"At the bottom of your garden, there is a river," the old man told the king. "Bathe in the river and the wish will be removed. All the things you touched will go back to how they were."

The king ran to the bottom of the garden and threw himself into the river. And when he looked up, he saw his daughter running and laughing in the garden.

And this made the king happier than he had ever been!

A national treasure is something an entire country values and protects. It might be an object, a person or a place.

Uluru is a national treasure in Australia. People travel from all over to see it. You can see why.

Find out about other national treasures. Which would you value the most? Why?

treasure

How to write about your opinion

State your opinion

Think about the main question in the introduction on page 4 of this book. What is your opinion?

Research

Look for other information that you need to back up your opinion.

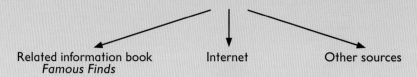

Related information book
Famous Finds

Internet

Other sources

Make a plan

Introduction

How will you "hook" the reader to get them interested?

Write a sentence that makes your opinion clear.

List reasons to support your opinion.

Support your reason
with examples.

Support your reason
with examples.

Support your reason
with examples.

Conclusion

Write a sentence that makes your opinion clear. Leave your reader with a strong message.

Publish

Publish your writing.

Include some graphics or visual images.